Shining

in the Son

an S. Delene Thomas Devotional

But grow in the grace
and knowledge
of our Lord
and Savior
Jesus Christ.
To Him be the glory
both now and forever.
Amen.

II Peter 3: 18

My thanks to those to whom I am indebted:

To Oma Lee for her love and acceptance, for sharing
    her heart with me
To Sherry, for her adventurous spirit
To Bitsy, for her perseverance even unto death
To Aleeta, for her creative energy and generous
    heart
To Mama, for her diligence in doing the hard
    things
To Ruth, for her inspiring faithfulness
To Nancy, for her friendship and for accepting me
    just as I am
To Missy and her family, for bringing great joy to
    my life
To Joey, for his love of God
To Julian, the love of my life and my friend

May the Lord bless and keep you all!

S. Delene Thomas
September 2020

SHINING IN THE SON

Then those who feared the Lord spoke to one another, and the Lord listened and heard them; so a book of remembrance was written before Him for those who fear the Lord and who meditate on His name. "They shall be Mine," says the Lord of hosts, "on the day that I make them My jewels. And I will spare them as a man spares his own son who serves him." Malachi 3: 16-17

You shall be called by a new name, which the mouth of the Lord will name. You shall also be a crown of glory in the hand of the Lord, and a royal diadem in the hand of your God. Isaiah 62: 2b-3

The Lord their God will save them in that day, as the flock of His people. For they shall be like the jewels of a crown. Zechariah 9: 16

Do you see yourself as the "jewel" that you are? Chosen in Him before the foundation of the world, He saw you complete and beautiful, a jewel in His crown.

When you first came to Him, you were in your raw state, just like a gem encased in a rock. He made your spirit brand new, but your soul needed His gentle touch to cut away the rough edges, creating the facets that catch His light. His creative love then polished the facets so that you shine in His hand.

Quite often we complain about the trials of life because we cannot see the process of our refinement.

1

If we could understand that He takes life's trials and uses them for our good, we could view them with joy. He does not cause the bad things we go through, but He does redeem them. He gives gifts that are good and perfect. He is working in you that you will be good and perfect – a gift to others and to Himself. He loves you!

For the things which are seen are temporary, but the things which are not seen are eternal.
II Corinthians 4: 18b

JESUS ONLY

When they had lifted up their eyes, they saw no one but Jesus only. Matthew 17: 8

How often have I looked around me at the world's offerings and become enticed, or, on my better days dismayed? The things of this world are temporary and the enjoyment of them is for a little while. They are hardly worth clinging to even momentarily, much less throwing one's whole life away in order to obtain them. I might think "Oh, if I only had this or that, why, I would be happy all my days!" But has not life shown me that even the best things of earth soon lose their charm? The soul becomes jaded and the beauty of the desired thing begins to pall. How fickle I am! When one thing's desirability fades, something else looms on the horizon and I am once again engaged in the pursuit of the new thing.

On the other hand, if I look at the world with other eyes, I might find myself becoming dismayed at the sordid nature of things, at the poverty, the pain, and the perversity. My soul is grieved and rightly so, if my grief leads me to action, if I step forward and change what I can in my sphere of influence. A word of encouragement, a gift of charity, meeting the need of another, lending a helping hand – these I can do and make someone's world a bit brighter.

I have found, however, if my focus is on the underbelly of life, I can become discouraged, and after a time, depressed. My small efforts do not seem to

3

help that much. There is always another mouth to feed, another soul to lift up, another trouble, another torment, another desperate need. My heart is broken again and again by the murder of unborn children, by the abuse and neglect of little ones. Even the scenes of abused animals can cause tears to come to my eyes. I cannot stop the terrible results of sin from occurring in this world. Mankind is becoming more depraved. Evil is multiplying exceedingly. Is it no wonder that the earth is groaning and that it must be purified with fire?

What is the balance then? *When they had lifted up their eyes, they saw no one but Jesus only.* Jesus Himself said that when we see the horrors coming on the earth to look up, for our redemption draws near.

Jesus is the only focal point that will keep me in balance. Neither the desire for material things and worldly pleasures nor the dismay and grief over the depravity I see will become too much for me to bear if I keep my eyes on Jesus. He is the Life, my Life, my Joy, my Peace, my All in all.

I can take His light wherever I go and change the atmosphere. I can share His joy with the hopeless, His life with the helpless, His peace with the restless, and His love with the unlovable and unlovely.

He is the lifter of my head!

In Him we live and move and have our being.
Acts 17: 28

Do not be overcome by evil, but overcome evil with good. Romans 12: 21

Now may the God of hope fill you with all joy and peace in believing, that you may abound in hope by the power of the Holy Spirit. Romans 15: 13

But You, O Lord, are a shield for me, my glory and the One who lifts up my head. Psalm 3: 3

But the day of the Lord will come as a thief in the night, in which the heavens will pass away with a great noise, and the elements will melt with fervent heat; both the earth and the works that are in it will be burned up. Therefore, since all these things will be dissolved, what manner of persons ought you to be in holy conduct and godliness, looking for and hastening the coming of the day of God, because of which the heavens will be dissolved, being on fire, and the elements will melt with fervent heat? II Peter 3: 10-12

Of old you laid the foundation of the earth, and the heavens are the work of Your hands. They will perish, but You will endure; yes, they will all grow old like a garment; like a cloak You will change them, and they will be changed. Psalm 102: 25-26

Lift up your eyes to the heavens, and look on the earth beneath. For the heavens will vanish away like smoke, the earth will grow old like a garment, and those who dwell in it will die in like manner;

but My salvation will be forever, and My righteousness will not be abolished. Isaiah 51: 6

For the creation was subjected to futility, not willingly, but because of Him who subjected it in hope; because the creation itself also will be delivered from the bondage of corruption into the glorious liberty of the children of God. For we know that the whole creation groans and labors with birth pangs together until now. Romans 8: 20-22

ARE YOU A STINKER?

Now thanks be to God who always leads us in triumph in Christ, and through us diffuses the fragrance of His knowledge in every place. For we are to God the fragrance of Christ among those who are being saved and among those who are perishing. II Corinthians 2: 14-15

How often when going about our daily lives do we find ourselves doing or saying something not very Christ-like? We find words coming from our mouths that should never be on the tongue of one who belongs to God's family. After all, we have the family name to uphold! Does not our gossip, slander, complaining, and dare I say, lying reflect badly on our Father and our Lord Jesus Christ? Is not the Holy Spirit within us grieved over our sin and carelessness? It is so easy to join in conversations that do not honor the law of love in Christ Jesus.

I find, as a Christian, that this is one of my greatest failings. I sometimes find myself engaged in the verbal assassination of someone's character, usually someone not present.

At other times, I complain about how life is treating me when I should be praising my Father because of His goodness. Isn't complaining a not so subtle way of blaming God for not giving me what I want when I want it? That is pretty blunt, but did not God punish Israel in their wilderness journey because of their complaining?

I am called to higher living than this. I am the fragrance of Christ in this world. The sweet smell of my life is supposed to encourage those who are being saved and reach out to the perishing to let them know that there is a better way, that there is hope.

For many years I have worn White Shoulders perfume. This has become my signature scent. People who hug me often say "You smell so good". Would that every person who comes near me experiences the fragrance of Christ and desires His presence in their own lives!

If I let down my guard and let the enemy in, then his foul smell permeates the atmosphere – I become a real stinker!

The Word says: *Let the word of Christ dwell in you richly in all wisdom, teaching and admonishing one another in psalms and hymns and spiritual songs, singing with grace in your hearts to the Lord. And whatever you do in word or deed, do all in the name of the Lord Jesus, giving thanks to God the Father through Him. Colossians 3: 16-17*

If I keep praising and singing priorites in my life, I cannot help but to live a sweet-smelling life through Jesus Christ my Lord. If I am always aware that others are watching and thereby "smelling" the odor of my life, then by the grace of God I can live a life well-pleasing to God and beneficial to those who come in contact with me. I can be a "perfume" of Christ and not a stinker!

IN MY FATHER'S HANDS

My sheep hear My voice, and I know them, and they follow Me. And I give them eternal life, and they shall never perish; neither shall anyone snatch them out of My hand. My Father, who has given them to Me, is greater than all; and no one is able to snatch them out of My Father's hand. John 10:27-29

How secure I am! I rest in my Father's hands. He who formed the worlds and all that exists holds me gently and tenderly in His mighty hands! Who can touch me there? Who would dare to confront my Father and try to wrest me from His hands of grace and mercy? What foul beast would try to tear me from His sheltering care? How foolish for any to even try! I am safe in my Father's hands!

Shall I be afraid of the snarling enemy who walks about as a roaring lion seeking whom he may devour? My Savior has broken the teeth of that prowling lion-pretender. Indeed, the Lion of Judah has triumphed over that old beast and has put him forever under His feet (and mine)! I am safe in my Father's hands!

These storms that arise – shall I fear their crashing waves and furious winds? When my little boat is riding up and down in the tempestuous sea, shall I be afraid? He made the seas, the clouds are merely the dust of His feet, the thunder is the sound of His mighty voice. Besides, He is in the boat with me and at the time of His choosing, He will heed my cry and will rise up and rebuke those

9

winds and waves. They will obey His voice for they too, know Him who is the Master of the seas, the Creator of heaven and earth. I am safe in my Father's hands!

These doubts, these nagging fears, these foolish worries – shall they separate me from my Father's loving hands? I think not! "Why are you so fearful?" Jesus asks. *Learn from Me the unforced rhythms of grace." (The Message)* Did I not say that whoever believes in Me shall never perish? Did I not tell you that I will be with you always? Did I not promise to supply all your needs? Did I not tell you that I am preparing a place for you and that I will come again and receive you unto Myself?

Fear, doubt, and fretfulness may come in for a brief visit, but by the grace of God, they shall not take up residence within me. I am the daughter of the King. I am chosen of God to be His very own. I am the temple of the living God, sealed by Holy Spirit Himself. I am in Christ Jesus and He is in me. I am safe in my Father's hands!

What kind of Father do I have? He is all powerful, all knowing, gracious, merciful, patient, kind, gentle, faithful, affirming, and loving. He does not just exhibit love, He is love! And He loves me! I am safe in my Father's hands!

How can I say so boldly that He loves me? He gave His only begotten Son to die a cruel death in my stead. And why? Certainly to atone for my sins, but more than that. He loved me from before the foundation of the world. God so loved. . .that He gave. Purely and simply, He wanted me for His own peculiar treasure. He wanted to be my Father. Because of His great love, I am His child, a citizen of the heavenly kingdom, and a king-priest here and now. I am an heir of God and He has promised to freely give me all things. He is a wonderful Father! He dearly loves me. I am safe in my Father's hands!

Do you know my Father?

Who shall separate us from the love of Christ? Shall tribulation, or distress, or persecution, or famine, or nakedness, or peril, or sword? As it is written: "For Your sake we are killed all day long; we are accounted as sheep for the slaughter". Yet in all these things we are more than conquerors through Him who loved us. For I am persuaded that neither death nor life, nor angels nor principalities nor powers, nor things present nor things to come, nor height nor depth, nor any other created thing, shall be able to separate us from the love of God which is in Christ Jesus our Lord. Romans 8: 35-39

The Lord is slow to anger and great in power, and will not at all acquit the wicked. The Lord has His way in the whirlwind and in the storm, and the clouds are the dust of His feet. Nahum 1: 3

For God so loved the world that He gave His only begotten Son, that whosoever believeth in Him should not perish but have everlasting life. John 3: 16 KJV

"I will be a Father to you, and you shall be My sons and daughters," says the Lord Almighty.
II Corinthians 6: 18

But God, who is rich in mercy, because of His great love with which He loved us, even when we were dead in trespasses, made us alive together with Christ (by grace you have been saved), and raised us up together, and made us sit together in the heavenly places in Christ Jesus, that in the ages to come He might show the exceeding riches of His grace in His kindness toward us in Christ Jesus.
Ephesians 2: 4-7

HIS YOKE IS EASY

Come to Me, all you who labor and are heavy laden, and I will give you rest. Take My yoke upon you and learn from Me, for I am gentle and lowly in heart, and you will find rest for your souls. For My yoke is easy and My burden is light. Matthew 11: 28-30

"Yoke" is a way of living, following the teachings and lifestyle of a rabbi. In Hebrew life, those who followed a rabbi were said to have taken his "yoke". They sat at his feet learning how to live. They gave up their own way to follow him and they watched him closely, following his example.

Jesus was often called "rabbi" or "teacher". His disciples followed Him to hear His teachings and to learn His way of living. They had taken His "yoke" upon themselves.

Jesus said that His way of living was easy. He would not lay heavy burdens on His followers, but would give them rest for their souls. Religion lays heavy burdens on us in the form of traditions and in a long list of dos and don'ts. This is a form of control. No matter how hard we strive to meet all the obligations of religion, we fail in one way or another or are just unable to do all the correct things in a consistent manner. As a result, we feel condemned, wearied in body and soul.

Jesus said that His yoke is gentle. Being the Good Shepherd that He is, He leads His sheep through the wilderness, the rough places, and the high mountains. The sheep's safety and well-being are in His hands. The sheep only needs to watch the Shepherd and walk where He walks. Only by straying from His chosen path will a sheep be in danger of harm from the treacherous elements that surround him. The Shepherd binds up the wounds when the sheep finds himself in places of brokenness and pain, He soothes the sheep with His voice and carries him tenderly until he is able to walk again. Along the pathway of His leading, the Good Shepherd provides green pastures of restoration in order that His flock can be renewed in strength and that the sheep can grow strong and fat and fruitful. He provides the living water of the Spirit to refresh and replenish the sheep. When times of darkness come, He causes His sheep to lie down under the starry heavens that He has created and there view His glory from a new perspective. When at long last their wanderings are over, He gathers His sheep into the sheepfold. Here the sheep are secure because Jesus Himself is the Door of the sheepfold and nothing nor no one can enter except other sheep who belong to Him.

Jesus said that He calls His own sheep by name and leads them out. And when He brings out His own sheep, He goes before them, and the sheep follow Him, for they know His voice. *Then Jesus said to them again, "Most assuredly, I say to you, I am the Door of the sheep. I am the Door. If anyone enters by Me, he will be saved, and will go in and out and find pasture. I have come that they may have life, and that they may have it more abundantly. I am the Good Shepherd. The Good Shepherd gives His life for the sheep. I am the Good Shepherd; and I know My sheep, and am known by My own. My sheep hear My voice, and I know them, and they follow Me. And I give them eternal life, and they shall never perish; neither shall anyone snatch them out of My hand. My Father, who has given them to Me, is greater than all; and no one is able to snatch them out of My Father's hand. John 10: 7, 9, 10b, 11, 14, 27-29*

What was Jesus' way of living, His "yoke"?

How God anointed Jesus of Nazareth with the Holy Spirit and with power, who went about doing good and healing all who were oppressed by the devil, for God was with Him. Acts 10: 38

Through His life, His acts, His teachings, His sacrificial death, Jesus came to show us the Father's heart of love and compassion. We were unable to get to the Father because of our sin, so He came to us through the Son and has made the Way for us. Jesus did everything necessary for our salvation. This gift of life is to be received – not by works, but by the grace of God extended to each of us. *For by grace you have been saved through faith, and that not of yourselves; it is the gift of God, not of works, lest anyone should boast. Ephesians 2: 8-9* Jesus said, *"Without Me you can do nothing." John 15: 5* That applies to salvation as well as our daily walk with Him. It is He who does the "work" in us. We are "channels only" as the old song says. We simply walk as He walked.

Walk worthy of the calling with which you were called, with all lowliness and gentleness, (just like Jesus, see Matthew 11: 28-30) *with longsuffering, bearing with one another in love, endeavoring to keep the unity of the Spirit in the bond of peace. Ephesians 4: 1b-3*

Therefore be imitators of God as dear children. And walk in love, as Christ also has loved us and given Himself for us, an offering and a sacrifice to God for a sweet-smelling aroma. Ephesians 5: 1-2

Walk as children of light (for the fruit of the Spirit is in all goodness, righteousness, and truth), finding out what is acceptable to the Lord. Ephesians 5: 8b-10

Being confident of this very thing, that He who has begun a good work in you will complete it until the day of Jesus Christ. Philippians 1: 6

For it is God who works in you both to will and to do for His good pleasure. Philippians 2: 13

MY LOVE, MY DOVE, MY FAIR ONE

One night as I was reading *Waking The Dead* by John Eldredge, I was reminded of God's words to me when I asked Him how He thought of me. He had answered "My dove, My fair one". Last night He said that I had missed part of it. He had actually said, "My love, My dove, My fair one". Even when He had been speaking those wonderful words, I had been unable to accept the fact that I am loved. Once again I wept at those affirming, tender words spoken by my Lord and my God.

I have never felt loved by anyone nor do I see myself as a gentle dove. I do see myself as ugly, so "fair one" is a surprise to me. Yet God sees me so differently than I see myself. He loves me even though He knows all about me. He sees every thought and understands every action. He sees the motives behind everything I say and do, and yet He loves me still!

Fact: I am loved by the Father and the Son.
He who has My commandments and keeps them, it is he who loves Me. And he who loves Me will be loved by My Father, and I will love him and manifest Myself to him. John 14: 21

Fact: I am espoused to Jesus Christ as His bride.
*For I am jealous for you with godly jealousy. For I have betrothed you to one husband, that I may present you as a chaste virgin to Christ.
II Corinthians 11: 2*

Fact: I am a member of God's family.

But as many as received Him, to them He gave the right to become children of God, to those who believe in His name. John 1: 12

For you are all sons of God through faith in Christ Jesus. Galatians 3: 26

Behold what manner of love the Father has bestowed on us, that we should be called the children of God! Therefore the world does not know us, because it did not know Him. Beloved, now we are children of God; and it has not yet been revealed what we shall be, but we know that when He is revealed, we shall be like Him, for we shall see Him as He is. I John 3: 1-2

Fact: I am indwelt by the Holy Spirit.

In Him you also trusted, after you heard the word of truth, the gospel of your salvation; in whom also, having believed, you were sealed with the Holy Spirit of promise, who is the guarantee of our inheritance until the redemption of the purchased possession, to the praise of His glory. Ephesians 1: 13-14

And because you are sons, God has sent forth the Spirit of His Son into your hearts, crying out, "Abba, Father!" Galatians 4: 6

Fact: I am the temple of God – the place where His shekinah glory dwells.

In whom the whole building, being fitted together, grows into a holy temple in the Lord, in whom you also are being built together for a dwelling place of God in the Spirit. Ephesians 2: 21-22

Do you not know that you are the temple of God and that the Spirit of God dwells in you?
I Corinthians 3: 16
Or do you not know that your body is the temple of the Holy Spirit who is in you, whom you have from God, and you are not your own?
I Corinthians 6: 19
For you are the temple of the living God.
II Corinthians 6: 16b

Fact: I am clothed in robes of righteousness given to me by Jesus Christ.
And be found in Him, not having my own right-eousness, which is from the law, but that which is through faith in Christ, the righteousness which is from God by faith. Philippians 3: 9
For He made Him who knew no sin to be sin for us, that we might become the righteousness of God in Him. II Corinthians 5: 21
But now the righteousness of God apart from the law is revealed, being witnessed by the Law and the Prophets, even the righteousness of God, through faith in Jesus Christ, to all and on all who believe. For there is no difference.
Romans 3: 21-22

Fact: I am part of the body of Christ – the Father loves the Son and I am part of His body, so the Father loves me just like He loves Jesus.
. . .holding fast to the Head, from whom all the body, nourished and knit together by joints and ligaments, grows with the increase that is from God. Colossians 2:19
But speaking the truth in love, may grow up in all things into Him who is the Head – Christ – from

whom the whole body, joined and knit together by what every joint supplies, according to the effective working by which every part does its share, causes growth of the body for the edifying of itself in love. Ephesians 4: 15-16

I in them, and You in Me; that they may be made perfect in one, and that the world may know that You have sent Me, and have loved them as You have loved Me. John 17: 23

Fact: I am in the process of going from glory to glory and the image of Jesus is being manifested in my life day by day as I grow to maturity in Him. I am filled with all the fullness of God.

But we all, with unveiled face, beholding as in mirror the glory of the Lord, are being transformed into the same image from glory to glory, just as by the Spirit of the Lord.
II Corinthians 3: 18

For whom He foreknew, He also predestined to be conformed to the image of His Son, that He might be the firstborn among many brethren.
Romans 8: 29

And of His fullness we have all received, and grace for grace. John 1: 16

To know the love of Christ which passes knowledge; that you may be filled with all the fullness of God. Ephesians 3: 19

Till we all come to the unity of the faith and of the knowledge of the Son of God, to a perfect man, to the measure of the stature of the fullness of Christ. Ephesians 4: 13

Not long ago I dreamed that I was looking into a mirror. It was large, oval in shape, and very ornate. The image I saw I recognized as myself. I was young and beautiful. I was astonished at what I saw. I particularly took note of my hair, and I tried to fix in my mind the way it was arranged so that when I woke up I might style it that way. As I thought on the meaning of the dream, I surmised that God had shown me what I would look like in eternity. Last night God reminded me of that dream and said that the image I saw was how He sees me now. He sees me apart from time; I am already that person to Him. *For the Lord does not see as man sees; for man looks at the outward appearance, but the Lord looks at the heart. I Samuel 16: 7* God sees the essential person inside of me. One day when this clay shell falls away, everyone will see that beautiful woman that I am. *So shall the King greatly desire thy beauty: for He is thy Lord; and worship thou Him. The King's daughter is all glorious within. Psalm 45: 11, 13 (KJV)*

*My Beloved spoke, and said to me: "Rise up, My love, My fair one, and come away.
Song of Solomon 2: 10*

I WILL GIVE YOU REST

Come to Me, all you who labor and are heavy laden, and I will give you rest. Take My yoke upon you and learn from Me, for I am gentle and lowly in heart, and you will find rest for your souls. For My yoke is easy and My burden is light. Matthew 11: 28-30

Through the finished work of the Lord Jesus Christ, I can be complete, whole – nothing missing, nothing broken. My part is to trust my Father to choose what path I must take to accomplish His design for my life. His desire for me is wholeness. He wants me to look and act like Jesus in all His ways. He is working in me moment by moment through the work of Holy Spirit to accomplish this task. I am admonished to take upon myself the "yoke" of the Lord Jesus and to walk in step with Him. As in the illustration of the Vine, I find that without Him I can do nothing. There is no strength, no vitality, nothing to cause me to flourish and grow, and produce fruit in myself. He does not call me to a set of laws that condemn me because I cannot do them, but He calls me to a relationship with Him in which He is my Friend, my Helper, my Shepherd, my All. I realize that He truly is my Life. Apart from Him I am and can do nothing. He invites me to this fellowship, this vital union with Him, and He promises me that His way of doing things (His yoke) is easy and His burden is light, easy to bear. There is no condemnation because He, having lived as one of us, knows how it is and that He made each of us to live in this vital union with Him. He has made it possible for us to become like Him, to share in His Father's family and house, to actually be "born ones" of the household of God. Is it not a small thing that He calls us to suffer for a little while that we might become more like Him and able to handle all the riches of our inheritance in Him and all the privileges of belonging to the family of God, sons and daughters of Almighty God?

But may the God of all grace, who called us to His eternal glory by Christ Jesus, after you have suffered a while, perfect, establish, strengthen, and settle you. I Peter 5: 10

Seeing then that we have a great High Priest who has passed through the heavens, Jesus the Son of God, let us hold fast our confession. For we do not have a High Priest who cannot sympathize with our weaknesses, but was in all points tempted as we are, yet without sin. Let us therefore come boldly to the throne of grace, that we may obtain mercy and find grace to help in time of need. Hebrews 4: 14-16

He is despised and rejected by men, a Man of sorrows and acquainted with grief. And we hid, as it were, our faces from Him; He was despised, and we did not esteem Him. Surely He has borne our griefs and carried our sorrows; yet we esteemed Him stricken, smitten by God, and afflicted. But He was wounded for our transgressions, He was bruised for our iniquities; the chastisement for our peace was upon Him, and by His stripes we are healed. All we like sheep have gone astray; we have turned, every one, to his own way; and the Lord

has laid on Him the iniquity of us all.
Isaiah 53: 3-6
For You have delivered my soul from death, my
eyes from tears, and my feet from falling. I will
walk before the Lord in the land of the living.
Psalm 116: 8-9

HANDCRAFTED OR HOMEMADE?

Handcrafted: fashioned with skill, artistry, and precision.
Homemade: made in the home; by one's own efforts; plain, simple or crude.

Being confident of this very thing, that He who has begun a good work in you will complete it until the day of Jesus Christ. Philippians 1: 6

I am assured that the salvation process that began at my new birth will be completed, not by my own works of righteousness, but with God's work in me through the Holy Spirit. He has not left me to my own devices any more than a mother would leave a newborn child. He knows our frame; He remembers that we are dust and without Him we can do nothing. This life-long process of sanctification has been planned before the foundation of the world and any good works that I may do are a manifestation of Christ in me. He knew that I could not save myself, neither could I behave myself, apart from Him. He placed the Holy Spirit in me at my new birth and it is through Him that I am enabled to do anything worthy of His kingdom and for His glory.

Just as He chose us in Him before the foundation of the world, that we should be holy and without blame before Him in love, having predestined us to adoption as sons by Jesus Christ to Himself, according to the good pleasure of His will, to the praise of the glory of His grace, by which He made us accepted in the Beloved. Ephesians 1: 4-6

Because He is God, He knew me and chose me for His own before He founded the world. It was no surprise to Him that sin would come into this world and that I would need a Savior. His plans were made long before the serpent entered the garden. He not only saw my need for a Savior, but also determined that I would be holy and blameless before Him because I stand in Christ's righteousness. I had none of my own; nothing to merit His great love and mercy. He did the choosing. He provided the perfect sacrifice for my sin. He put His Holy Spirit in me to seal me as His own but also to empower me to grow. He has determined that I should become like Jesus. He wanted me to be His daughter and to be with Him for all eternity. Could I merit this? No, by no means! He chose, He predestined, He made me accepted. It is His work on my behalf. Why? Love. There could be no other motivation.

But we are bound to give thanks to God always for you, brethren beloved by the Lord, because God from the beginning chose you for salvation through sanctification by the Spirit and belief in the truth, to which He called you by our gospel, for the obtaining of the glory of our Lord Jesus Christ. II Thessalonians 2: 13-14

The theme is repeated: God chose, from the beginning, for salvation and sanctification. He called me when I heard the gospel message. All glory to God and to His Son, Jesus Christ my Lord!

For You formed my inward parts; You covered me in my mother's womb. I will praise You, for I am

*fearfully and wonderfully made; marvelous are
Your works, and that my soul knows very well. My
frame was not hidden from You, when I was made
in secret, and skillfully wrought in the lowest
parts of the earth. Your eyes saw my substance, being yet unformed. And in Your book they all were
written, the days fashioned for me, when as yet
there were none of them. Psalm 139: 13-16
But when it pleased God, Who separated me from
my mother's womb and called me through His
grace, to reveal His Son in me. . .
Galatians 1: 15-16*

God saw me when I was being formed in my
mother's womb. He saw me, called me for His
own, and set me on the path that would lead me
to Him. He wants to reveal His Son in me, so I am
being shaped by those things God allows in my
life so that I shall be conformed to the image of
Jesus Christ. I share in the suffering He endured
and I shall also share in the power of His resur-
rection as God works in my life. I am to let Him do
His work in me, not striving to get out of the diffi-
cult places, but to learn from them so that His Son
may be seen in my life.

*For in Him dwells all the fullness of the Godhead
bodily; and you are complete in Him, who is the
head of all principality and power.
Colossians 2: 9-10*

I am complete in Him. All that I need is already
there in Him. The things of this world are going to
burn up; they have no lasting appeal. Any good
that I might do in myself will also burn up as

wood, hay, and stubble at the judgment seat of Christ. He is all I need.

I was birthed by the Holy Spirit of God. He is the power in me to change me from glory to glory and to take me from faith to faith. How could I ever think that this faulty flesh can have value? This house of flesh shall pass away so that I might be housed in the body that is like Christ's. That house is not made with hands and is eternal, heavenly (II Corinthians 5: 1). To even try to go about trying to establish my own righteousness is ludicrous. I have none! I am to simply work out what Christ Jesus has put in – to let the Light in me shine forth so that my Father is glorified.

I am His workmanship. He has prepared good works for me to walk in. In Christ Jesus I am alive to God and by His grace and mercy I am enabled to do those things for which He has called me. He gives me the power to do them so all the glory belongs to Him.

My complete sanctification is based on God's faithfulness to His Word. He will see to it that I am blameless in the day of my Lord Jesus Christ. How can this be? Because I will stand in His robe of righteousness, not in any homemade garments of my own efforts. I thank my Father that He has and is handcrafting me with infinite skill, perfect precision, and intricate, beautiful artistry!

WHEN STORMS COME

(written October 2004 after three hurricanes had devastated our city)

Immediately Jesus made His disciples get into the boat and go before Him to the other side, while He sent the multitudes away. And when He had sent the multitudes away, He went up on the mountain by Himself to pray. Now when evening came, He was alone there. But the boat was now in the middle of the sea, tossed by the waves, for the wind was contrary. Now in the fourth watch of the night Jesus went to them, walking on the sea. And when the disciples saw Him walking on the sea, they were troubled, saying, "It is a ghost!" And they cried out for fear. But immediately Jesus spoke to them, saying, "Be of good cheer! It is I; do not be afraid." And Peter answered Him and said, "Lord, if it is You, command me to come to You on the water." So He said, "Come." And when Peter had come down out of the boat, he walked on the water to go to Jesus. But when he saw that the wind was boisterous, he was afraid; and beginning to sink he cried out, saying, "Lord, save me!" And immediately Jesus stretched out His hand and caught him, and said to him, "O you of little faith, why did you doubt?" And when they got into the boat, the wind ceased. Then those who were in the boat came and worshiped Him, saying, "Truly You are the Son of God." Matthew 14: 22-33

Thoughts after the storm:

Throughout the past few months, we have faced many storms. The waves of life have been boisterous. Physical and mental energies have been drained. There is an ever present temptation to yield to fear. But there is good news. Jesus is here and He steps in immediately and stretches out His hand at our cry "Lord, save me!" Even as we are walking by faith as Peter was doing, answering Jesus' command to "come to Me", we might find ourselves overwhelmed by present circumstances. We do not have the time nor the words for long, elaborate prayers. Imagine what would have happened to Peter if he had tried to sound "religious": "Most gracious Lord, creator of the universe. . .glub, glub, glub.

No, in the urgency of his need, his heart cry was simply, "Lord, save me!" May we always be real with God and simply tell Him our hearts. He knows our needs even before we ask and He is willing and able to take care of anything we commit to Him.

STUCK ON THE WORD

Has the Lord ever promised you something and then made you wait a long time to receive it? Did you wait a week, a month, a year, ten years? Are you still waiting?

At such times it is easy to question. Did God really say this to me? Or, to ask yourself, "Am I doing something wrong or am I just not perfect enough so that I am preventing God from keeping His word to me?" After all, you reason, God cannot lie and He can do the impossible, so there must be something wrong with me. Then the Enemy comes along and whispers, "Don't you think God has had enough time to fulfill His promise? You missed it and He isn't going to come through for you." If he can get you to doubt, then he can begin to erode your faith. If you are not careful, you can allow anger to enter your heart. You can slip so far as to say, "If God couldn't keep this promise, then maybe He can't keep any other." At that point you are on shaky ground indeed! The Enemy's lies will utterly defeat you if you quit believing what God has said.

In recent days I heard a message that went straight to my heart and my need regarding this problem. The speaker did not know me from Adam, but God put in her mouth a message just for me. I have been waiting for the fulfillment of a promise God made to me years ago. I have been assailed by the Enemy day after day telling me to give up. The message I heard a few days ago was "never give up". The time of waiting on God is a fruitful time, a growing time. I do not want to miss the present blessings by having my attention fixed on that long-ago promise. The Word of God is true and I can rely on God's faithfulness.

I was reminded of the story in II Samuel 23: 10 that tells of King David's mighty men. It reads: *He arose and attacked the Philistines until his hand was weary, and his hand stuck to the sword. The Lord brought about a great victory that day; and the people returned after him only to plunder.*

The Lord challenged me to be like this man. Though his hand grew weary in fighting the enemies of the Lord, he held on until his hand stuck to the sword. The word stuck is translated in the King James Version as clave, the Hebrew word *dabaq*, meaning to stick, to adhere (like glue). It is the same word used in Genesis 2: 24 . . .a man shall cleave unto his wife and they shall be one flesh. I am to hold so tightly to the Word of God which is the sword of the Spirit, that I am stuck to it as though glued to it. I am to become one with it. When I hold on to the Word of God, I can expect, in God's time, to see the result that is recorded in this verse: *The Lord brought about a great victory that day.*

My challenge is this: hold on tight to the Word, the written Word and the Word who became flesh, Jesus Christ. This is my life and my victory — I can't let go no matter what!

FIGHTING THE GOOD FIGHT

Be sober, be vigilant; because your adversary the devil walks about like a roaring lion, seeking whom he may devour. I Peter 5: 8

Because our adversary is aggressively hostile, we as Christians are to be spiritually alert, not only to withstand his attacks, being fully clothed with the armor of God, but by prayer and spiritual warfare opposing him.

We are warned that Satan goes about like a roaring lion. The lion, when he hunts, looks for the weak, the young, the isolated, the unguarded; they are marked for attack. The Devil's ultimate agenda is to kill and destroy us if possible. He will maim, hurt, and discourage those who are not watchful.

We are not left alone to fight him, but have been given the full armor of God. It is not just passive protection, but it is to be used aggressively against the unseen spiritual forces that oppose us. Paul's admonition to us is *praying always with all prayer and supplication in the Spirit, being watchful to this end with all perseverance and supplication for all the saints. Ephesians 6: 18*

Prayer is the means by which we engage in the battle and the purpose for which we are armed. To put on the armor of God is to prepare for the battle. Prayer is the battle itself, with God's Word being our chief weapon against Satan during the struggle. We see this in Jesus' temptation. Again and again He answered Satan, saying *It is written. . .* Continuous prayer *(praying always)* is necessary because spiritual warfare is continuous. We need the prayer for ourselves and as Paul reminds us, for all the saints.

We are not alone in the battle, for Jesus promised *I am with you always. Matthew 28: 20.* Paul tells us to *Be strong in the Lord and in the power of His might Ephesians 6: 10. For the weapons of our warfare are not carnal but mighty in God II Corinthians 10: 4. We are more than conquerors through Him who loved us Romans 8: 37.*

We have everything we need as soldiers of the cross:

- The power of God, through the indwelling Holy Spirit John 14: 16-17; Acts 1: 8
- The perfect love of God, poured out in our hearts, to cast out fear I John 4: 18; Romans 5: 5
- The abiding presence of Jesus Christ who gives us the victory I John 5: 4-5; I Corinthians 15: 57
- The mind of Christ so that we walk in the ways of God and make sound choices I Corinthians 2: 16; Philippians 2: 5; Romans 12: 2
- The authority of Jesus Christ over all the power of the enemy Luke 10: 19

Watch, stand fast in the faith, be brave, be strong. Let all that you do be done with love. Therefore, my beloved brethren, be steadfast, immovable, al-

*ways abounding in the work of the Lord, knowing
that your labor is not in vain in the Lord.
I Corinthians 16: 13-14; 15: 58*

*Finally, my brethren, be strong in the Lord and in
the power of His might. Put on the whole armor of
God, that you may be able to stand against the
wiles of the devil. For we do not wrestle against
flesh and blood, but against principalities, against
powers, against the rulers of the darkness of this
age, against spiritual hosts of wickedness in the
heavenly places. Therefore take up the whole armor of God, that you may be able to withstand in
the evil day, and having done all, to stand. Stand
therefore, having girded your waist with truth,
having put on the breastplate of righteousness,
and having shod your feet with the preparation of
the gospel of peace; above all, taking the shield of
faith with which you will be able to quench all the
fiery darts of the wicked one. And take the helmet
of salvation, and the sword of the Spirit, which is
the word of God; praying always with all prayer
and supplication in the Spirit, being watchful to
this end with all perseverance and supplication
for all the saints. Ephesians 6: 10-18*

*For the weapons of our warfare are not carnal but
mighty in God for pulling down strongholds, casting down arguments and every high thing that exalts itself against the knowledge of God, bringing
every thought into captivity to the obedience of
Christ. II Corinthians 10: 4-5*

*What then shall we say to these things? If God is
for us, who can be against us? He who did not*

spare His own Son, but delivered Him up for us all, how shall He not with Him also freely give us all things? Who shall bring a charge against God's elect? It is God who justifies. Who is he who condemns? It is Christ who died, and furthermore is also risen, who is even at the right hand of God, who also makes intercession for us. Who shall separate us from the love of Christ? Shall tribulation, or distress, or persecution, or famine, or nakedness, or peril, or sword? As it is written: "For Your sake we are killed all day long; we are accounted as sheep for the slaughter". Yet in all these things we are more than conquerors through Him who loved us. For I am persuaded that neither death nor life, nor angels nor principalities nor powers, nor things present nor things to come, nor height nor depth, nor any other created thing shall be able to separate us from the love of God which is in Christ Jesus our Lord. Romans 8: 31-39

For whatever is born of God overcomes the world. And this is the victory that has overcome the world – our faith. Who is he who overcomes the world, but he who believes that Jesus is the Son of God? I John 5: 4-5

For God has not given us a spirit of fear, but of power and of love and of a sound mind. II Timothy 1: 7

Means of warfare:

- Diligent, earnest prayer; seeking after God, searching with all your heart Jeremiah 29: 11-14
- Fasting Ezra 8: 21 – 23; Mark 9: 14-29
- Tears Psalm 126: 5-6
- Taking authority in the spiritual realm Luke 10: 19
- Physical acts prompted by faith and motivated by a genuine intensity of prayer II Kings 19: 8-19
- Vocal praise and shouting I Samuel 4: 5-6; I Kings 1: 40
- Lifting hands and bowing heads Nehemiah 8: 6
- Dancing and leaping Psalm 149: 3; Luke 6: 23
- Groaning in prayer Romans 8: 23; Galatians 4: 19

THE CHILDREN'S BREAD AND GENTILE DOGS

Then Jesus went out from there and departed to the region of Tyre and Sidon. And behold, a woman of Canaan came from that region and cried out to Him, saying, "Have mercy on me, O Lord, Son of David! My daughter is severely demon-possessed." But He answered her not a word. And His disciples came and urged Him, saying, "Send her away, for she cries out after us." But He answered and said, "I was not sent except to the lost sheep of the house of Israel." Then she came and worshiped Him, saying, "Lord, help me!" But He answered and said, "It is not good to take the children's bread and throw it to the little dogs." And she said, "Yes, Lord, yet even the little dogs eat the crumbs which fall from their masters' table." Then Jesus answered and said to her, "O woman, great is your faith! Let it be to you as you desire." And her daughter was healed from that very hour. Matthew 15: 21-28

From there He arose and went to the region of Tyre and Sidon. And He entered a house and wanted no one to know it, but He could not be hidden. For a woman whose young daughter had an unclean spirit heard about Him, and she came and fell at His feet. The woman was a Greek, a Syro-Phoenician by birth, and she kept asking Him to cast the demon out of her daughter. But Jesus said to her, "Let the children be filled first, for it is not good to take the children's bread and throw it to the little dogs." And she answered and said to Him, "Yes, Lord, yet even the little dogs under the table eat

from the children's crumbs." Then He said to her,
"For this saying go your way; the demon has gone
out of your daughter." And when she had come to
her house, she found the demon gone out, and her
daughter lying on the bed.
Mark 7: 24-30

For years I have been putting myself in the role of
the woman who begged for crumbs, but I was
putting myself in the wrong place. I am not a Gen-
tile dog begging for the crumbs, but a child of God
seated at His table with bread in abundance. This
woman was asking for healing and Jesus said it
was the children's bread and that they should be
filled. Healing and bread are related in this passage.

David said *I have been young, and now am old; yet*
I have not seen the righteous forsaken, nor his de-
scendants begging bread. Psalm 37: 25.

I am clothed in Christ's righteousness, a child of
God by faith in Jesus Christ, born again from
above, of the seed of Abraham by faith, and an
heir to the promises to him and his seed, a joint
heir with Jesus Christ. I am both "the righteous"
and "the descendant", so I need not beg for bread
any longer. All that I need is already mine in
abundance. I just need to partake of it, freely and
joyfully with a heart of thanksgiving.

Righteousness, cleansing, health, wholeness –
whatever kind of bread I need is available to me
anytime. Christ Jesus, the Bread of Life, is in me
and I am in Him. All of His abundance is mine!

I have been begging for that which is already mine. I just had not recognized nor received it. It is available to me in the same way salvation was available, a gift to be received. God gave me the faith to receive His gift of salvation. No works that I could do could ever earn that salvation. It is His gift to me.

In the same way, all my striving to earn His other gifts to me just caused me confusion, frustration, and weariness of soul. I cannot do anything to make myself worthy of any of God's blessings. He has made me worthy and I receive His gift by the faith He has given me – no more begging and no more striving by my own works to receive.

Thanks be to God for His grace freely given to me so that I may live a life of wholeness, abundance, and wellness. I receive Your gift, Father God, and I bless Your name for Your patience with me as I was learning this lesson.

Bless the Lord, O my soul; and all that is within me, bless His holy name! Bless the Lord, O my soul, and forget not all His benefits: Who forgives all your iniquities, Who heals all your diseases, Who redeems your life from destruction, Who crowns you with lovingkindness and tender mercies, Who satisfies your mouth with good things, so that your youth is renewed like the eagle's.
Psalm 103: 1-5

THE FAITH OF ABRAHAM AND ANSWERED PRAYER

And he believed in the Lord, and He accounted it to him for righteousness. Genesis 15: 6

Therefore it is of faith that it might be according to grace, so that the promise might be sure to all the seed, not only to those who are of the law, but also to those who are of the faith of Abraham, who is the father of us all (as it is written, "I have made you a father of many nations") in the presence of Him whom he believed – God, who gives life to the dead and calls those things which do not exist as though they did; who, contrary to hope, in hope believed, so that he became the father of many nations, according to what was spoken, "So shall your descendants be". And not being weak in faith, he did not consider his own body, already dead (since he was about a hundred years old), and the deadness of Sarah's womb. He did not waver at the promise of God through unbelief, but was strengthened in faith, giving glory to God, and being fully convinced that what He had promised, He was also able to perform. And therefore "it was accounted to him for righteousness".
Romans 4: 16-22

And if you are Christ's, then you are Abraham's seed, and heirs according to the promise.
Galatians 3: 29

I have been thinking for several weeks about the faith of Abraham. We know that Abraham believed God and his faith was accounted to him for righteousness. How was Abraham's faith expressed?

First, he left his home and family to go out to a land that he did not know. At the word of the Lord, he left his comfort zone.

Secondly, he believed God would give him a son and make of him a great nation even though the circumstances made this look impossible.

Thirdly, when the Lord told him to offer that promised son as a burnt offering, he prepared to obey, believing that God was able to raise him from the dead. God had asked him, *"Is anything too hard for the Lord?"* Abraham replied, "No, nothing is too hard for Him."

In Luke 1: 37 an angel said to Mary, *"For with God nothing will be impossible."* The prophet Jeremiah declared in Jeremiah 32: 17: *"Ah, Lord God! Behold, You have made the heavens and the earth by Your great power and outstretched arm. There is nothing too hard for You."* Jesus speaks in Luke 18: 27: *The things which are impossible with men are possible with God."*

Jesus also tells us: *". . .whatever you ask the Father in My name He will give you. Until now you have asked nothing in My name. Ask and you will receive, that your joy may be full." John 16: 23-24 "Ask, and it will be given to you; seek, and you will find; knock, and it will be opened to you. For everyone who asks receives, and he who seeks finds, and to him who knocks it will be opened. Or what man is there among you who, if his son asks for bread, will give him a stone? Or if he asks for a fish, will he give him a serpent? If you then, being evil, know how to give good gifts to your children, how much more will your Father who is in heaven give good things to those who ask Him!" Matthew 7: 7-11 "Therefore I say to you, whatever things you ask when you pray, believe that you receive them, and you will have them." Mark 11: 24*

The promises arc true, we would never say otherwise, yet we don't receive what we ask for. Why not?

Some would say that these promises were spoken only to the twelve apostles. After all, they needed to do miracles to authenticate their word in preaching the Gospel. However, miracle-working power was given to the seventy also. *Behold, I give you the authority to trample on serpents and scorpions, and over all the power of the enemy, and nothing shall be any means hurt you. Nevertheless do not rejoice in this, that the spirits are subject to you, but rather rejoice because your names are written in heaven. Luke 10: 19-20*

Philip the evangelist was not an apostle, yet he cast out demons and healed the sick (Acts 8: 7). His four daughters prophesied (Acts 21: 9). Paul and Barnabas both did signs and wonders though Barnabas was not an apostle (Acts 14: 3; 15: 12).

That was the first century some people would claim. Yet Jesus said after giving the Great Commission: *And these signs will follow those who be-*

lieve: in My name they will cast out demons; they will speak with new tongues; they will take up serpents; and if they drink anything deadly, it will by no means hurt them; they will lay hands on the sick, and they will recover. Mark 16: 17-18

Jesus said in John 14: 12-14: *Most assuredly, I say to you, he who believes in Me, the works that I do he will do also; and greater works than these he will do, because I go to My Father. And whatever you ask in My name, that I will do, that the Father may be glorified in the Son. If you ask anything in My name, I will do it.*

The one who believes Jesus, in whatever age he lives, can take these promises as his own.

Many believe that the day of miracles has passed. The argument is that they were only needed in the first century to authenticate the Word. We have the completed Old and New Testaments now. Yet church history shows that raising the dead and healing the sick were common until the fourth century. Miracles occur today. The secular news media does not report them, but they do happen.

My daughter's church in California has seen three miraculous answers to prayer in recent times: a woman with a brain tumor was healed, a man with pancreatic cancer, given less than three months to live, was healed, and my own granddaughter was born healthy and whole even though she was wrapped in her umbilical cord and the cord had a tight knot in it. In Naples,

Florida my daughter and I stayed with Christian friends, Miriam and Gideon. Gideon told us about his friend Bill, son of a Baptist minister. God called Bill to be a missionary/evangelist to Mexico. He traveled from village to village preaching to the poor. Early in his ministry, in the village where he was, a young man drowned. Bill heard God tell him to raise the young man from the dead. Being like you and me, Bill said, "Lord, I can't do that. If I fail, the people will not listen to me any longer." Bill knew immediately that he had failed God. Later he found himself in a similar situation and God again told him to raise the person from the dead. And he did! Since that time, Bill has been used of God again and again to raise the dead. In one village, a woman had two daughters who died at the same time. Because of their poverty, she wrapped them in cloth and placed them in a burial pit for paupers and they were covered with lime. She then went to find the missionary and by the time they returned to her village, the girls had been dead for four days. Bill prayed over them and they rose to life again. At another village where he was preaching, he was almost overcome by a horrible stench in the air. He finally asked someone what the awful smell was and they pointed to a canvas-covered heap nearby. The Lord directed Bill to go and look under the canvas. He did not want to do so, but he did obey. Beneath the cloth was a hideous mass of rotting flesh – a leper. The nose was completely gone and the cheeks were fallen away also. The whole body was terrible to behold. God said to Bill, "Lay your hands on him and pray for his healing." After a short argument with God, Bill prayed for the man. His hands sank into the man's chest. Bill was fearful of contracting leprosy and as soon as possible he washed himself thoroughly and left the village. Some time later, he returned to the village and was met by a crowd of people smiling and beckoning to him to "come and see". A young man ran up to him and took his hands. He thanked Bill profusely. Bill said, "Do I know you?" The young man said, "Yes, you prayed for me when you were here before – I was that leper!" The man was now handsome and whole. His nose was beautifully formed and his skin had a healthy glow.

I know of other reports from missionaries and evangelists who have seen miraculous healings, have witnessed the dead raised to life, and who have themselves spoken in languages that they have never studied. Why do we not see these things happen in our churches?

Jesus had the answer in Matthew 17: 20: *So Jesus said to them, "Because of your unbelief; for assuredly, I say to you, if you have faith as a mustard seed, you will say to this mountain, 'Move from here to there', and it will move; and nothing will be impossible for you." And the apostles said to the Lord, "Increase our faith." So the Lord said, "If you have faith as a mustard seed, you can say to this mulberry tree, 'Be pulled up by the roots and be planted in the sea', and it would obey you." Luke 17: 5-6*

But, you would say, it might not be God's will to do what I ask. If your request does not violate the Word of God, then ask! God responds to faith. *But without faith it is impossible to please Him, for he who comes to God must believe that He is, and that He is a rewarder of those who diligently seek Him. Hebrews 11: 6*

The only limitations I see are our lack of faith and our lack of diligence in seeking the Lord. Through the Word and by spending time in His presence, we can know Him and know His will. We can then be confident in prayer. If we are serious about prayer, we need to believe God's Word on the subject. We have the privilege of coming boldly before the throne of grace. Let's just ask what we will and leave the answers in God's hands. Don't limit God because of unbelief. Don't limit Him by not asking what you will. Let it not be said of us as was said of some in Matthew 13: 58: *Now He did not do many mighty works there because of their unbelief.* Let us also not be among those mentioned in James 4: 2: *You do not have because you do not ask.* We are the seed of Abraham – believe God!

THE UNSHAKABLE KINGDOM

But now He has promised saying, "Yet once more I shake not only the earth, but also heaven." Now this "yet once more", indicates the removal of those things that are being shaken, as of things that are made, that the things which cannot be shaken may remain. Hebrews 12: 26-27

They shall go into the holes of the rocks, and into the caves of the earth, from the terror of the Lord and the glory of His majesty, when He arises to shake the earth mightily. Isaiah 2: 19

For thus says the Lord of hosts: Once more (it is a little while) I will shake heaven and earth, the sea and dry land, and I will shake all nations. Haggai 2: 6-7

The heavens and earth will shake; but the Lord will be a shelter for His people. Joel 3: 16

The earth itself is shaking. There are reports almost every week of earthquakes all over the earth, even in places that are not known for them. Not too long ago there were nine quakes in two days in Irving, Texas of all places! Scientists predict that a quake is coming to the center of the United States that will divide it into two land masses. Cities along the Mississippi River are preparing for this to happen. Scientists say that a massive quake is long overdue that will devastate the state of California. Jesus told us that in the last days there would be earthquakes in various places.

Nations are shaking. There are wars in many nations right now and preparations are being made for war in many other nations. Our own nation is in turmoil because of racial tensions and because of the worldwide pandemic. Terrorist groups are threatening to destroy the United States and Israel.

The structures of society are shaking. Government at all levels is being undermined by corruption and moral decay. Business is in upheaval because of bribery, greed, and closures due to the pandemic. Society at large is marked by crime, racism, and debauchery. Our children are not safe in school or even in their own beds. Our churches are divided along denominational lines, decimated and weakened by legalism and liberalism, and destroyed by gross sin in the ranks. Our homes are torn by divorce and child abuse. Children are killing parents and parents are killing children.

These are grim realities indeed! But there is hope! As Christians we are subjects of a heavenly kingdom. Jesus Christ Himself reigns over this kingdom. His kingdom is not yet that of the earth, the stumbling block of the Jews in the first century. They knew that the Christ would come as a child and even knew where He would be born. They knew He would rule over the earth and set them free from their enemies. But they did not know that these were two separate events. Jesus came the first time to gain the victory over the devil, over sin, and over death. In the future millennial kingdom, He will reign as King of kings and Lord of lords and every knee will bow to Him and every tongue will confess that He is Lord.

What is the kingdom of God? Jesus spoke often of this kingdom and gave many illustrations of its nature. He compared it to a sower sowing seeds, to wheat and tares, to a mustard seed, to leaven, to hidden treasure, to a pearl, to a net, to a king settling his accounts, to a landowner hiring laborers, to a king arranging a marriage for his son, to ten virgins waiting for the bridegroom, and to a man traveling to a far country.

Basically a kingdom is a dominion or territory over which a king rules. The sphere of God's rule is the idea of the kingdom we think of most often. He is sovereign and rules over all His creation.

There is the kingdom that is to come where Jesus will reign over the earth. He will reign over all peoples and His kingdom will never end.

Presently the kingdom is active in the heart of each believer. It is within us. The evidence of the kingdom within is spoken of in Romans 14: 17; *the kingdom of God. . . is righteousness and peace and joy in the Holy Spirit.* If Jesus Christ is reigning in my heart, these things should be evident. No matter what is shaking around me, the kingdom within is unshakable, because the Prince of Peace rules there.

Therefore, since we are receiving a kingdom which cannot be shaken, let us have grace, by which we may serve God acceptably with reverence and godly fear. Hebrews 12: 28

GOD CAME NEARER

One of the most widely held beliefs in Christendom is the omnipresence of God. This means that He is present in all places at all times. Because of who God is, we know that He cannot be contained. He fills all that exists.

The omnipresence of God was recognized by men of old. *"Am I a God near at hand," says the Lord, "and not a God afar off? Can anyone hide himself in secret places, so I shall not see him?" says the Lord. "Do I not fill heaven and earth?" says the Lord. Jeremiah 23: 23-24*

Where can I go from Your Spirit? Or where can I flee from Your presence? If I ascend into heaven, You are there; if I make my bed in hell, behold, You are there. If I take the wings of the morning, and dwell in the uttermost parts of the sea, even there Your hand shall lead me, and Your right hand shall hold me. If I say, "Surely the darkness shall fall on me", even the night shall be light about me; indeed, the darkness shall not hide from You, but the night shines as the day; the darkness and the light are both alike to You."
Psalm 139: 7-12

But will God indeed dwell on the earth? Behold, heaven and the heaven of heavens cannot contain You. How much less this temple which I have built! I Kings 8: 27

Though He is everywhere, men of old were privileged to walk and talk with Him. Adam and Eve walked with Him in the garden. Enoch walked with God and one day God took him home to be with Him. Noah and Abraham walked and talked with Him. Moses saw Him in a burning bush; he talked with Him on the mountain, and he saw the back of Him while in that mountain alone with Him. He appeared in fire by night and a cloud by day to all the Israelites. His shekinah glory was seen over and inside the tabernacle and in the temple. Isaiah saw *the Lord sitting on a throne, high and lifted up, and the train of His robe filled the temple. Isaiah 6: 1* Though these men and women enjoyed a rare and great privilege, they could not hold Him. The moment always came that He departed from them.

Then came an appointed time when He came nearer than David, Solomon, or Jeremiah could ever imagine. *Behold, the virgin shall be with child, and bear a Son, and they shall call His name Immanuel, which is translated "God with us". Matthew 1: 23*

There are many wondrous things about the Christmas story. Men and angels interacted face to face and in dreams. Shepherds heard and saw the angels of God on the wonderful night when God came near. God, in the form of a baby, came down to dwell among us. As John the Beloved puts it, *the Word became flesh and dwelt among us, and we beheld His glory, the glory as of the only begotten of the Father, full of grace and truth. John 1: 14*

Why did He come? He came to reveal the Father. He wanted to show us the reality and the character of God. And, He came to die on an old rugged cross so that we might be redeemed. He shed His blood to make atonement for our sins. He ascended to the right hand of the Father, and there He is our mediator. But did you know that God came even nearer?

The mystery which has been hidden from ages and from generations, but now has been revealed to His saints. To them God willed to make known what are the riches of the glory of this mystery among the Gentiles: which is Christ in you, the hope of glory. Colossians 1: 26-27

At that day you will know that I am in My Father, and you in Me, and I in you. John 14: 20

Jesus answered and said to him, "If anyone loves Me, he will keep My word; and My Father will love him, and We will come to him and make Our home with him." John 14: 23

I in them, and You in Me; that they may be made perfect in one, and that the world may know that You have sent Me, and have loved them as You have loved Me. And I have declared to them Your name, and will declare it, that the love with which You loved Me may be in them, and I in them. John 17: 23, 26

But you are not in the flesh but in the Spirit, if indeed the Spirit of God dwells in you. Now if anyone does not have the Spirit of Christ, he is not

His. And if Christ is in you, the body is dead because of sin, but the Spirit is life because of righteousness. But if the Spirit of Him who raised Jesus from the dead dwells in you, He who raised Christ from the dead will also give life to your mortal bodies through His Spirit who dwells in you.
Romans 8: 9-11

Or do you not know that your body is the temple of the Holy Spirit who is in you, whom you have from God, and you are not your own?
I Corinthians 6: 19

You are of God, little children, and have overcome them, because He who is in you is greater than he who is in the world. I John 4: 4

We shall never be parted from Him, for He promised to never leave us or forsake us.

GOD IS WITH US! GOD IS IN US! These are truly tidings of great joy. Tell someone today the glorious message of Jesus Christ – the One who dwells within!

WHAT BATTLE?

For You have armed me with strength for the battle. Psalm 18: 39

Do you ever have the feeling that there is more going on around you than meets the eye? Do you wonder why your prayers don't seem to get answered? Or why God's people act in such ungodly ways? Do you ever feel that there must be someone who is out to bring you down?

There is such an enemy of your soul who wants to prevent you from fulfilling God's plan for your life. His name is Satan. He cannot destroy your eternal soul, but he can make you an ineffective Christian. He is after you, your family, your church, and every other thing that is God's. Jesus said that our enemy came *to steal, and to kill, and to destroy John 10: 10.*

There is a war going on around us and each one of us has a vital part in it.

There is an interesting passage in Daniel 10: 12-13: *Then he said to me, "Do not fear, Daniel, for from the first day that you set your heart to understand, and to humble yourself before your God, your words were heard; and I have come because of your words. But the prince of the kingdom of Persia withstood me twenty-one days; and behold, Michael, one of the chief princes, came to help me, for I had been left alone there with the kings of Persia."*

Daniel's prayer was heard but the answer was delayed three weeks because the evil angelic being who had authority over Persia fought with the angel of God who had been sent to Daniel. The angel called for Michael, a chief angel, for help to overcome the evil being. If angels must have help to overcome the enemy, how much more do you or I?

In Ephesians 6: 10-12 we are admonished: *Finally, my brethren, be strong in the Lord and in the power of His might. Put on the whole armor of God, that you may be able to stand against the wiles of the devil. For we do not wrestle against flesh and blood* (people are not your enemy), *but against principalities, against powers, against the rulers of the darkness of this age, against spiritual hosts of wickedness in the heavenly places.*

We learn in II Corinthians 10: 3-5: *For though we walk in the flesh, we do not war according to the flesh. For the weapons of our warfare are not carnal but mighty in God for pulling down strongholds, casting down arguments and every high thing that exalts itself against the knowledge of God, bringing every thought into captivity to the obedience of Christ.*

Note that our strength is "in the Lord", we fight "in the power of His might", and our armor is "of God". God has equipped us for battle. We are urged *to endure hardship as a good soldier of Jesus Christ II Timothy 2: 3. We are urged to withstand in the evil day, and having done all to stand. Stand, therefore, having girded your waist with truth, having put on the breastplate of right-*

eousness, and having shod your feet with the preparation of the gospel of peace; above all, taking the shield of faith with which you will be able to quench all the fiery darts of the wicked one. And take the helmet of salvation, and the sword of the Spirit, which is the word of God; praying always with all prayer and supplication in the Spirit, being watchful to this end with all perseverance and supplication for all the saints. Ephesians 6: 13-18

We stand fully equipped for war. Retreat is unthinkable. So *fight the good fight of faith I Timothy 6: 12.* God *gives us the victory through our Lord Jesus Christ I Corinthians 15: 57.* Jesus said, *All power (authority) has been given to Me in heaven and on earth Matthew 28: 18.* We have the Holy Spirit with us. *Greater is He that is in you than he that is in the world I John 4: 4.* And we know that *we are more than conquerors through Him who loved us Romans 8: 37.*

So then, *we are persuaded that neither death nor life, nor angels nor principalities nor powers, nor things present nor things to come, nor height nor depth, nor any other created thing shall be able to separate us from the love of God which is in Christ Jesus our Lord. Romans 8: 38-39*

Someday the battles will be over and all the spoils of victory will be ours. In that day *God will wipe away every tear from their eyes; there shall be no more death, nor sorrow, nor crying. There shall be no more pain, for the former things have passed away. And there shall be no more curse, but the throne of God and of the Lamb shall be in it, and*

His servants shall serve Him. They shall see His face, and His name shall be on their foreheads. There shall be no night there. They need no lamp nor light of the sun, for the Lord God gives them light. And they shall reign forever and ever. Revelation 21: 4; 22: 3-5.

Hallelujah! Amen!

LIVING FROM YOUR HEART

Keep your heart with all diligence, for out of it spring the issues of life. Proverbs 4: 23

Eight hundred ninety-seven verses in the King James Bible speak of the heart. The heart can be broken, hardened, full of enmity, grieved, perverse, offended, confused, deceived, deceitful, prideful, uncircumcised, slow to believe, and divided. But the heart can also be courageous, glad, merry, generous, tender, creative, compassionate, refreshed, faithful, full of faith, and believing.

OUT OF THE HEART COMES THE MOTIVES FOR THE THINGS WE SAY AND DO.
Jesus said, *"Out of the abundance of the heart the mouth speaks." Matthew 12: 34.* This same thought is found in Luke 6: 45: *A good man out of the good treasure of his heart brings forth good; and an evil man out of the evil treasure of his heart brings forth evil. For out of the abundance of the heart his mouth speaks.*

THE MOTIVES OF THE HEART DETERMINE THE INTEGRITY OF ONE'S LIFE.
Jesus said in Luke 8: 15: *"Those who, having heard the word with a noble and good heart, keep it and bear fruit with patience."* Note II Timothy 2: 22: *Pursue righteousness, faith, love, peace with those who call on the Lord out of a pure heart.* Also Hebrews 10: 22 *Let us draw near with a true heart in full assurance of faith, having our hearts sprinkled from an evil conscience and our bodies*

washed with pure water. A heart that is noble, good, pure, and true – that is a treasure worth having!

IN THE HEART WE THINK OUR DEEPEST THOUGHTS.

But Mary kept all these things and pondered them in her heart. Luke 2: 19

My son, give attention to my words; incline your ear to my sayings. Do not let them depart from your eyes; keep them in the midst of your heart; for they are life to those who find them, and health to all their flesh. Proverbs 4: 20-22

Wisdom rests in the heart of him who has understanding. Proverbs 14: 33

The heart of the righteous studies how to answer. Proverbs 15: 28

Let the words of my mouth and the meditation of my heart be acceptable in Your sight, O Lord, my strength and my Redeemer. Psalm 19: 14

The meditation of my heart shall give understanding. Psalm 49: 3

I applied my heart to know, to search, and seek out wisdom and the reason of things. Ecclesiastes 7: 25

A wise man's heart discerns both time and judgment. Ecclesiastes 8: 5

FROM OUR HEART COMES OUR CREATIVITY.

I have put wisdom in the hearts of all the gifted artisans. Exodus 31: 6

And all the women whose hearts stirred with wisdom spun yarn of goat's hair. Exodus 35: 26

Then Moses called Bezalel and Aholiab, and every gifted artisan in whose heart the Lord had put wisdom, everyone whose heart was stirred, to come and do the work. Exodus 36: 2

God gives creativity to the heart. Use that creativity for His glory.

COURAGE IS FOUND IN THE HEART

Though an army may encamp against me, my heart shall not fear. Psalm 27: 3

And he shall say to them, Hear, O Israel: Today you are on the verge of battle with your enemies. Do not let your heart faint, do not be afraid, and do not tremble or be terrified because of them. Deuteronomy 20: 3

Wait on the Lord; be of good courage, and He shall strengthen your heart. Psalm 27: 14

Let not your heart be troubled. . .neither let it be afraid. John 14: 1, 27

Courage arises from the heart when the heart is trusting in God.

THE HEART IS THE RECEPTACLE OF MEMORY

We are to store our memories of what God has said and what He has done in our lives so that we might keep His Word and teach others also.

Only take heed to yourself, and diligently keep yourself, lest you forget the things your eyes have seen, and lest they depart from your heart all the days of your life. And teach them to your children and your grandchildren. Deuteronomy 4: 9

And these words which I command you today shall be in your heart. Deuteronomy 6: 6

Therefore you shall lay up these words of mine in your heart and in your soul. Deuteronomy 11: 18

IT IS IN THE HEART THAT OUR FAITH IN CHRIST ARISES.

Heart belief, not head knowledge, will bring salvation to the soul.

That if you confess with your mouth the Lord Jesus and believe in your heart that God has raised Him from the dead, you will be saved. For with the heart one believes unto righteousness, and with the mouth confession is made unto salvation. Romans 10: 9-10

Then Philip opened his mouth and beginning at this Scripture, preached Jesus to him. Now as they went down the road, they came to some water. And the eunuch said, "See, here is water. What hinders me from being baptized?" Then Philip said, "If you believe with all your heart, you may." And he answered and said, "I believe that Jesus Christ is the Son of God." Acts 8: 35-37

IT IS IN THE HEART THAT WE ENJOY INTIMATE FELLOWSHIP WITH GOD.

God wants to dwell with us, talk with us, and fill us with His fullness – it is a matter of the heart.

Seek the Lord your God, and you will find Him if you seek Him with all your heart and with all your soul. Deuteronomy 4: 29

Then you will call upon Me and go and pray to Me, and I will listen to you. And you will seek Me and find Me, when you search for Me with all your heart. Jeremiah 29: 12-13

And because you are sons, God has sent forth the Spirit of His Son into your hearts, crying out, "Abba, Father!" Galatians 4: 6

That Christ may dwell in your hearts through faith; that you, being rooted and grounded in love, may be able to comprehend with all the saints what is the width and length and depth and height – to know the love of Christ which passes knowledge; that you may be filled with all the fullness of God. Ephesians 3: 17-19

John Eldredge puts it so well: "The Bible sees the heart as the source of all creativity, courage, and conviction. It is the source of our faith, our hope, and of course, our love. It is the "wellspring of life" within us, the very essence of our existence, the center of our being, the fount of our life. You cannot be the person God meant you to be, and you cannot live the life He meant you to live unless you live from the heart."*

Your heart matters – it is your life!

Waking The Dead, John Eldredge, Nelson Books, 2003, pp. 40, 49

DON'T GROW WEARY

Recently a verse from the book of Joshua caught my eye. In chapter 11, verse 18, we read: *Joshua made war a long time with all those kings.* At the beginning when Joshua led the children of Israel against Og and Sihon on the other side of Jordan and then crossed over into the Promised Land to fight against Jericho, I am sure Joshua was encouraged because of the victories won, especially the unusual victory over Jericho. I wonder how he felt years later after long years of warfare? Did he have the same enthusiasm? The same anticipation of victory over the enemy? The same joy when victory was won? He came to old age and there was very much land yet to be possessed (Joshua 13: 1). Did the enormity of the task discourage Him? I wonder.

Has your journey been long? How are you faring? Is your enthusiasm waning? Do victories seem few and far between? Are you becoming weary in well-doing?

The Lord is aware of our tendency to become weary and complacent. We are admonished concerning this very thing:
And let us not grow weary while doing good, for in due season we shall reap if we do not lose heart. Galatians 6: 9
I know your works, your labor, your patience... and you have persevered and have patience, and have labored for My name's sake and have not become weary. Nevertheless, I have this against you, that you have left your first love. Remember there-

65

fore from where you have fallen; repent and do the first works. Revelation 2: 2-5

Those addressed here have persevered, they have patience, they have labored, and have not become weary, yet they have lost the enthusiasm they had at the beginning.

Do you find yourself as I sometimes do, falling into this category? I am doing the right things and saying the right words; I am "keeping on keeping on", yet I have lost the joy, the excitement, the "first love".

We know that we are called to be faithful and that we are co-workers with Christ. We know that our works will be judged and that the field of our labor is ready to be harvested. We know the coming of the Lord is near. We know these things and yet we let ourselves become careless and lackadaisical. How thankful I am for a loving Father who remembers that we are dust and that He has infinite patience!

There is a scene in the movie *Narnia: The Lion, The Witch, and The Wardrobe* that encourages my heart when I think of the calling of the Lord to labor and to wage war against the enemy. Lucy and her older sister, Susan, have just witnessed the death of Aslan by the hand of Jadis, the White Witch. They have wept over his broken, dead body and have fallen asleep from grief and weariness. They wake at dawn and are dismayed to find that Aslan's body is gone. Suddenly Aslan appears, in all of his glory and majesty, standing in the archway, alive and shining in the sun! Their joy knows no bounds as they rush to him and bury their faces in his mane, hugging him and laughing. Aslan touches them with his tongue (lion kisses) and laughs with them. After a time he tells them that the battle has been joined and it is time to go. He does not force them to go alone, he is going with them. He does not require them to run in their own strength, he carries them on his back. He has already supplied them with weapons – Lucy's healing potion and Susan's bow and arrows. They run toward the battle armed, unafraid, and assured of victory because Aslan is with them. Can we not go forward in like manner – fully armed, confident, and compelled by the love of Christ, knowing that our victory is sure because He has already won?

THE LORD MY SHIELD

The Lord is my rock and my fortress and my deliverer; my God, my strength, in whom I will trust; my shield and the horn of my salvation, my stronghold. Psalm 18: 2

The Lord is my strength and my shield; my heart trusted in Him, and I am helped; therefore my heart greatly rejoices, and with my song I will praise Him. Psalm 28: 7

For the Lord God is a sun and shield; the Lord will give grace and glory; no good thing will He withhold from those who walk uprightly. Psalm 84: 11

You are my hiding place and my shield; I hope in Your word. Psalm 119: 114

Every word of God is pure; He is a shield to those who put their trust in Him. Proverbs 30: 5

The Lord has not left me defenseless against the attacks of the enemy. I do not stand alone. I do not rely on my puny strength. I dare not! My faith, which is a gift from Him, has placed me in Christ Jesus, protected by the Father and secure in His hand. Nothing can touch me except it first go through my Father. He shields me with Himself. Every part of me is covered and safe.

How is it then that the enemy so often hits me with his fiery darts? In my naiveté and in my pride, I strike out on my own, exposing myself to danger. I forget that apart from Him I can do nothing. What arrogance I find in myself at times and then how I do howl when I am struck by the enemy! How gracious is my God and Father who hears my cry for help and comes to my rescue again and again. He does not turn away when I call. He forgives me fully when I repent and ask for forgiveness.

Why do I not remember that I am safe when I am close to Him? When I submit to God and resist the devil, the devil must flee from me. He sees that God is my shield and he knows that he has been defeated. The closer that I move toward God, the closer He moves toward me. When I am surrounded by my Shield, I am secure. He protects every part of me – my mind, my body, my soul. Inside my Strong Tower, I can dwell safely. Inside the defense He has built for me, I find peace, security, joy, and His loving presence. Why would I ever want to be anywhere else?

ZEPHANIAH 3: 17

The Lord your God in your midst, The Mighty One, will save; He will rejoice over you with gladness, He will quiet you with His love, He will rejoice over you with singing. Zephaniah 3: 17

Recently I had one of those days. I felt terrible, there were many heavy burdens that I just could not seem to leave at Jesus' feet, I could not see even a candle in the darkness. I sat down to read my Bible, intending to turn to Isaiah 53, a chapter I was memorizing. It was one of those moments when your Bible opens elsewhere to just the passage that is needed in a dark hour. My Bible fell open to the last chapter of Zephaniah. The seventeenth verse leaped off the page and I started to cry.

God is so good! He knows just what to say and just when to say it. I had read the verse many times before, even had it underlined, but that moment the *logos* (written word) became a *rhema* (personal word). As I meditated on the verse, I began to put it in a context that was meaningful to me. Because I have had no positive father-figure in my life, I often have trouble thinking of God as my Father in positive ways. But the verse did mean a great deal more to me by thinking of it in terms of being a mother and a grandmother. Part of the verse says *He will rejoice over you with gladness.* I thought of the first time I held my children or my granddaughters. How gladness had filled my heart as I thought of the miracle that I held and rejoiced that this little one was whole and healthy. My heavenly Father looks at me with that same tenderness and joy. He is glad that I am His!

The next part of the passage says *He will quiet you with His love.* That was just what I needed that troubled morning. I thought of the times I had held a fretful baby in my arms, how I gently patted and stroked its tiny back, and crooned soft, sweet sounds to the little one until the baby relaxed and the fretting ceased. God my Father wanted to do that for me. What a thought! He is called *the God of all comfort.*

Finally, the verse says, *He will rejoice over you with singing.* How precious and awesome is the thought that the God of the universe, the Creator and Sustainer of all that exists, the great I AM, wants to sing over me. I thought of the hours I have held my little ones in a rocking chair or on a porch swing singing to them for hours. They loved it and so did I. My heavenly Father wants to quiet me by drawing me to Himself and cause me to think on His great love. Then, and only then, can I be still and know that He is God. He has everything under control and He has His eye on me. He will never leave me nor forsake me. He holds me in His hand. Oh, that I can be still enough to hear Him singing over me!

THE LORD THINKS ABOUT ME

The Lord takes thought and plans for me.
Psalm 40: 17 (Amplified)

For I know the thoughts and plans that I have for
you, says the Lord, thoughts and plans for welfare
and peace and not for evil, to give you hope in your
final outcome. Jeremiah 29: 11 (Amplified)

What an awesome thought it is that Almighty God
– Jehovah – the great I AM thinks about me and
weaves the events of my life together. I only see
the underside of the beautiful tapestry He is
weaving, but the day is coming when I shall see
that *all things work together for good to those who*
love God, to those who are the called according to
His purpose. Romans 8: 28

Because He knows all things concerning me, I am
assured that:

HE KNOWS MY PAIN
The Lord is close to those who are of a broken heart
and saves such as are crushed with sorrow. Psalm
34: 18 Amplified
This is my comfort and consolation in my afflic-
tion: that Your word has revived me and given me
life. Psalm 119: 50 Amplified
You have turned my mourning into dancing for
me. You have put off my sackcloth and girded me
with gladness. Psalm 30: 11
He not only sees my pain, but because He is the
God of all comfort and the God who heals, He has
the remedy for my pain and I have His promise

that He will take care of it if I will allow Him access to my heart.

HE KNOWS MY FEARS
God is our Refuge and Strength, a very present help in trouble. Therefore we will not fear. Psalm 46: 1-2

For God has not given us a spirit of fear, but of power and of love and of a sound mind. II Timothy 1: 7

I sought the Lord, and He heard me, and delivered me from all my fears. Psalm 34: 4

By trusting in His Word and relying on the Lord completely, the things that cause me to fear seem less intimidating and I am, in time, delivered from those very fears – all of them!

HE KNOW MY WEAKNESSES
O God, You know my folly and blundering; my sins and my guilt are not hidden from You. Psalm 69: 5 Amplified

My flesh and my heart fail; but God is the strength of my heart and my portion forever. Psalm 73: 26

Likewise the Spirit also helps in our weaknesses. Romans 8: 26

And He said to me, "My grace is sufficient for you, for My strength is made perfect in weakness." Therefore most gladly I will rather boast in my infirmities, that the power of Christ may rest upon me. II Corinthians 12: 9

He gives power to the weak, and to those who have no might He increases strength. Even the youths shall faint and be weary, and the young men shall utterly fall, but those who wait on the Lord shall renew their strength; they shall mount up with

wings like eagles, they shall run and not be weary, they shall walk and not faint. Isaiah 40: 29-31
God will strengthen me in my weakness or will use that weakness to bring glory to Himself.

HE KNOWS THE LONGINGS OF MY HEART
O Lord, You have heard the desire and the longing of the humble and the oppressed; You will prepare and strengthen and direct their hearts. You will cause Your ear to hear. Psalm 10: 17 Amplified
Delight yourself also in the Lord, and He shall give you the desires of your heart. Psalm 37: 4
For He satisfies the longing soul, and fills the hungry soul with goodness. Psalm 107: 9
There is nothing hidden from His eyes and He delights in giving. I can trust Him with my secret desires.

HE SEES MY TEARS
The Lord has heard the voice of my weeping. Psalm 6: 8
You number and record my wanderings; put my tears into Your bottle – are they not in Your book? Psalm 56: 8 Amplified
He will surely be gracious to you at the sound of your cry; when He hears it, He will answer you. Isaiah 30: 19 Amplified
And God will wipe away every tear from their eyes; there shall be no more death, nor sorrow, nor crying. There shall be no more pain, for the former things have passed away. Revelation 21: 4
As a tender, loving Father, God sees my tears. He comforts me now and someday He will wipe away my tears forever.

HE SEES THE BURDENS THAT I CARRY

Cast your burden on the Lord, and He shall sustain you. Psalm 55: 22

Casting all your care upon Him, for He cares for you. I Peter 5: 7

Come to Me, all you who labor and are heavy laden, and I will give you rest. Matthew 11: 28

God never meant for me to bear heavy burdens, but to lay them down at His feet, trusting Him to take care of any distressing situation facing me.

HE SEES MY DISTRESS

I will be glad and rejoice in Your mercy and steadfast love, because You have seen my affliction. You have taken note of my life's distresses.
Psalm 31: 7 Amplified

In my distress I called upon the Lord, and cried out to my God; He heard my voice from His temple, and my cry came before Him, even to His ears. Psalm 18: 6

In my distress I cried to the Lord, and He heard me. Psalm 120: 1

When I call for help, my Father hears and answers.

HE REMEMBERS MY FRAME

As a father pities his children, so the Lord pities those who fear Him. For He knows our frame; He remembers that we are dust. Psalm 103: 13-14

As I think on the goodness of the Lord to me, I ask myself, "What should be my response?" The Word has the answer for me:

Praise the Lord! Sing to the Lord a new song, and His praise in the assembly of saints. Let Israel rejoice in their Maker; let the children of Zion be joyful in their King. Let them praise His name with the dance; let them sing praises to Him with the timbrel and harp. For the Lord takes pleasure in His people; He will beautify the humble with salvation. Let the saints be joyful in glory; let them sing aloud on their beds. Let the high praises of God be in their mouth, and a two-edged sword in their hand. Psalm 149: 1-6

Joy, singing, praising, dancing, holding to the Word of God, blessing the Lord, loving Him supremely, being thankful, giving Him glory, and worshiping Him in holiness – these are the ways I can respond to His gracious, loving heart. God the Omnipotent, the Almighty, the Holy One, the One like no other, thinks about me. Hallelujah!

GREAT IS THY FAITHFULNESS

Through the Lord's mercies we are not consumed, because His compassions fail not. They are new every morning; great is Your faithfulness. Lamentations 3: 22-23

Your mercy, O Lord, is in the heavens; Your faithfulness reaches to the clouds. Psalm 36: 5

I will sing of the mercies of the Lord forever; with my mouth will I make known Your faithfulness to all generations. For I have said, Mercy shall be built up forever; Your faithfulness You shall establish in the very heavens. And the heavens will praise Your wonders, O Lord: Your faithfulness also in the assembly of the saints. O Lord God of hosts, who is mighty like You, O Lord? Your faithfulness also surrounds You. Psalm 89: 1-2, 5, 8

Your faithfulness endures to all generations. Psalm 119: 90

Do you notice a theme? Today I am thinking of the faithfulness of God. Every close relationship is founded on faithfulness. God's covenants are as sure as His faithfulness. We can trust Him because He has proven Himself faithful.

The Hebrew word *emunah* is the noun form of faithfulness meaning "certainty". The synonyms are: righteousness, lovingkindness, and justice. They are often listed together in Scripture. The verb form is *aman*, meaning "to be certain, enduring, to trust, to believe". Three words come from this verb form: true, faithful, amen. Does that sound like Someone you have heard of and know?

These things says the Amen, the Faithful, and True Witness, the Beginning of the creation of God. Revelation 3: 14

Jesus is faithful. We can count on Him. He does not just have the trait of faithfulness, He is faithfulness. He is the Amen. Faithfulness is an essential part of God. We can rely on every word He says. He cannot lie. He will do what He says.

I heard an old adage once that said: He who is born of God is certain to resemble his Father. We, by the power of the Holy Spirit working in us, are to reflect this character trait of God. Does faithfulness characterize your life? Can you be counted on to honor your word even if it requires unexpected effort? Do you resemble your Father?

But the fruit of the Spirit is love, joy, peace, long-suffering, kindness, goodness, faithfulness, gentleness, self-control. Galatians 5: 22-23a

BLESSED QUIETNESS

Be still and know that I am God. Psalm 46: 10

The Lord is good to those who wait for Him, to the soul who seeks Him. It is good that one should hope and wait quietly for the salvation of the Lord. Lamentations 3: 25-26

Be silent in the presence of the Lord God. Zephaniah 1: 7

Stand still and consider the wondrous works of God. Job 37: 14

Meditate within your heart on your bed, and be still. Psalm 4: 4

It is beneficial to just be still before the Lord, to think about Him, and to listen to what He wants to say to us. In our world where everyone is in a hurry and anything and everything is instant – from coffee to sending messages – it is a rare thing to find a space and time for quietness. The opportunity won't just happen. We have to decide to be still before the Lord. The benefits of doing so are great.

In quietness and confidence shall be your strength. Isaiah 30: 15

The work of righteousness will be peace, and the effect of righteousness, quietness and assurance forever. My people shall dwell in a peaceful habi-

tation, in secure dwellings, and in quiet resting places. Isaiah 32: 17-18

And Moses said to the people, "Do not be afraid. Stand still, and see the salvation of the Lord, which He will accomplish for you today. For the Egyptians whom you see today, you shall see again no more forever. The Lord will fight for you, and you shall hold your peace." Exodus 14: 13-14

And Moses said to them, "Stand still, that I may hear what the Lord will command concerning you." Numbers 9: 8

Now therefore, stand still, that I may reason with you before the Lord concerning all the righteous acts of the Lord which He did to you and to your fathers. I Samuel 12: 7

You will not need to fight in this battle. Position yourselves, stand still and see the salvation of the Lord, who is with you. . .do not fear or be dismayed. . .the Lord is with you. II Chronicles 20: 17
The benefits received from quietness before the Lord indicated in these verses are:

- Strength and confidence
- Assurance, peace, rest
- Instruction from the Lord
- Knowledge of the greatness and goodness of God
- A reminder of the wonderful things He has done
- Freedom from fear in the face of trial
- Knowledge that the Lord is with you

With benefits like these, would it not be worth-while to find the time every day to be still before the Lord without voicing any petitions to Him, but just waiting in quietness before Him until you are filled with the assurance that HE IS! When that thought captures your heart and mind, the troubles of this world will be dwarfed by the greatness of our God. Your heart and mind can rest securely just because HE IS!